You Can Be Whatever You Wallaby!

By Christopher Clements

Copyright © 2021 by Christopher Clements

All rights reserved. This book or any portion thereof may not be reproduced or used in any manner whatsoever without the express written permission of the author, with the exception of small portions for review purposes.

Hey!

Can you be a firefighter? An artist?
A chef? An accountant?

Of horse you can!

Don't cry fowl!

I'm not lion.

With lots of aard-vark, you can do anything!

And if you don't like where you're at,
it's never too late to try something elk.

Spend time with deer friends.

Share with otters.

Savor moo-ments,
big and small.

And hug your mole family!

When you're feeling down,
look to those who love you.

You're never koala-lone.

An opportunity to try gnu things!

To bull-ieve in yourself!

To gopher gold!

A chance to be whatever you wallaby!

The End.

Made in the USA
Middletown, DE
25 July 2022